WHAT DO YOU KNOW ABOUT

EVOLUTION
AND CLASSIFICATION

ANNA CLAYBOURNE

PowerKiDS
press

Published in 2018 by **The Rosen Publishing Group, Inc.**
29 East 21st Street, New York, NY 10010

CATALOGING-IN-PUBLICATION DATA

Names: Claybourne, Anna.
Title: What do you know about evolution and classification? / Anna Claybourne.
Description: New York : PowerKids Press, 2018. | Series: Test your science skills | Includes index.
Identifiers: ISBN 9781538323021 (pbk.) | ISBN 9781538322093 (library bound) | ISBN 9781538323038 (6 pack)
Subjects: LCSH: Evolution (Biology)--Juvenile literature. | Evolution--Juvenile literature. | Animals--Classification--
  Juvenile literature.
Classification: LCC QH367.1 C627 2018 | DDC 576.8--dc23

Series Editor: Amy Pimperton
Series Designer: Emma DeBanks
Picture Researcher: Diana Morris

Picture credits: Alexkalina/Dreamstime: 20t. Andamanec/Shutterstock: 21bl. Marcel Baumgartner/Shutterstock: 12t. catmando/Shutterstock: 5br. CNRI/SPL: 18cr. Paul Crash/Shutterstock: 3bc. Stephen Dalton/NHPA/Photoshot/Avalon: 8b. Andrea Dant/Shutterstock: 18b. DimaSid/Shutterstock; 16c. dovia982/Shutterstock: 11cr. Dziewul/Shutterstock: 12b, 29t. Elliflamra/istockphoto: 10c. Diek Ercken/Shutterstock: 6c. Erni/Shutterstock: 14t. Ex0rzist/Shutterstock: 21bc. Friedemeier/Dreamstime: 22t. Julien Grondin/Dreamstime: 23t. Steve Gschmeissner/SPL/Alamy: 10b.Henrikhi/ Dreamstime: 21brl Oliver Hoffmann/Shutterstock: 17t. Dieter Hopf/Imagebroker/FLPA: 5tr:Hugoht/Dreamstime: 22cl. Interfoto/Alamy: 9b.Isselee/Dreamstime: 5tr: Brian A Jackson/Shutterstock: 1, 18t. MCY Jerry/CC Wikimedia Commons: 4tr:Varin Jindawong/Shutterstock: 21bcr. JPL Designs/Shutterstock: 20ca. Kamonrat/Shutterstock: 24bc. Maksim Kazaov, Hein Nouwens, Igor Petrovic,Tristan Tan/Shutterstock: 21c. Kochergin/Shutterstock: 15bl. Vitaly Korovin/Shutterstock: 29b. KTS Design/SPL: front cover. Richard Laskowski/Dreamstime: 9t.LifeTimeStock/Shutterstock: 15t. Lukas ZB/ Shutterstock: 11b. S & D Maslowski/FLPA: 14bl. redrawn from de Muizon C, Nature 413. © Macmillan 2001: 14cr. NaturesMomentsuk/Shutterstock: 21t. Nopainnogain/Shutterstock: 26t. Ali Ozgurdonmaz/Getty Images: 13c. Picture Researchers/FLPA: 14bc. Nataly Ponomarenko/Shutterstock: 28b. Alexander Potapov/Shutterstock: 24bl. PrimePhoto/ Shutterstock: 16b. Ondrej Prosicky/Shutterstock: 12c. Redline Vector/Shutterstock: 19t. Revers/Shutterstock: 25b. Arie van'T Riet/SPL: 3br. D Roberts/SPL: 24t. Susan Robinson/Dreamstime: 5tc. Andres Rodriguez/Dreamstime: 21br. M Rutherford/Shutterstock: 20cb.Andrew Sabai/Shutterstock: 6cr. Dario Sablijak/Shutterstock: 4bl. Sanpom/Shutterstock: 16t.Kevin Schafer/Minden Pictures/FLPA: 17b. Svetlana Serebryakova/Shutterstock: 27t. Andrei Shumskiy/Shutterstock: 7r. Sombra/Shutterstock: 6t. Maurus Spescha/Shutterstock: 15bc. Sinclair Stammer/SPL: 22b. Stephen Sweet/ Dreamstime: 6b. Szeno/Dreamstime: 22cr. Evgeny Tomeev/Shutterstock: 25t. Vlodymyr Tsyba/Dreamstime: 5bl. Thierry Vialard/Dreamstime: 18cl. Olga Visavi/Shutterstock: 20c. vitstudio/Shutterstock: 7b, 27b. whiteisthecolor/Shutterstock: 11c. CC Wikimedia Commons: 8t, 8ca, 10t. David Wingate/Shutterstock: 15br. Martin B Withers/FLPA: 8c. Rudmer Zwerver/Shutterstock: 14cl. Zyancarlo/Shutterstock: 26b.

Manufactured in China

CPSIA Compliance Information: Batch BW18PK: For Further Information contact Rosen Publishing, New York, New York at 1-800-237-9932.

CONTENTS

Worlds in **bold** can be found in the glossary on page 30.

A note about measurements
Measurements are given in U.S. form with metric in parentheses. The metric conversion is rounded to make it easier to measure.

WHAT IS EVOLUTION?

Evolution is a process of gradual change. In science, it means the way different types, or **species**, of living things change over time.

The world has millions of different species of animals, plants, **bacteria**, and other living things. They have evolved over millions of years to become the way they are today. For example, today's horses evolved from a much smaller animal — *Hyracotherium*.

This diagram shows some of the stages in the evolution of the modern horse.

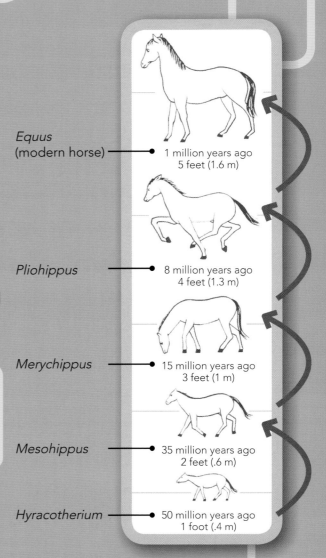

Equus (modern horse) — 1 million years ago 5 feet (1.6 m)

Pliohippus — 8 million years ago 4 feet (1.3 m)

Merychippus — 15 million years ago 3 feet (1 m)

Mesohippus — 35 million years ago 2 feet (.6 m)

Hyracotherium — 50 million years ago 1 foot (.4 m)

HABITATS AND SURVIVAL

Evolution happens because all living things, even if they belong to the same species, are different. Those that are best at surviving in their surroundings, or **habitat**, tend to live longer and **reproduce** more often.

This happens by chance and is not deliberate. But it means that each species evolves to become better at surviving in its habitat.

Mushrooms have evolved to suit damp, shady habitats.

NATURAL SELECTION

Here's an example of how evolution works.

1. These rabbit kits (babies) are all the same species, but they have slight differences. For example, some might have stronger back legs and run faster. Faster rabbits are more likely to escape from **predators**, such as red foxes.

2. This means they will be more likely to grow up and have their own babies.

When animals have babies, they often pass on their features to them. So rabbits with strong back legs will become more common, while the weaker ones die out.

3. Over time, the species changes and all rabbits become faster runners. This process is called **natural selection**. The best survivors are "selected" by nature.

red fox

rabbit running

rabbit kits

EXTINCT AND NEW SPECIES

As well as evolving, living things sometimes struggle to survive. This means their species can die out, or become **extinct**.

Meanwhile, more species can develop. Sometimes, one species divides into separate groups. They can evolve in different ways to become two or more new species.

Dinosaurs died out about 65 million years ago.

Scientists have discovered thousands of species of **reptiles**, both extinct and living today. They include snakes, lizards, and dinosaurs.

THE SCIENCE OF EVOLUTION

The word science means "knowledge." So science simply means finding things out. Scientists have been studying our world and the creatures in it for thousands of years.

Studying evolution is one of the most important parts of **biology**, the science of life. It helps us to understand why living things, including humans, are the way they are today.

The axolotl is an **amphibian** related to newts and frogs. Its Latin name is *Ambystoma mexicanum*.

WHAT'S WHAT?

Classification is an essential part of science too. It explains the relationships between living things. When scientists discover a new species, they classify it and give it its own scientific name in **Latin**. This means that scientists around the world, who speak different languages, always know which species they are talking about.

newt

frog

USEFUL KNOWLEDGE

The study of evolution also helps with other areas of science. For example, it helps us fight diseases, such as the flu, by learning how disease **germs** evolve. In **geology**, the science of rocks, understanding how life evolved helps scientists work out how old rocks are.

Tiny flu **viruses** can only be seen through a microscope.

WORKING SCIENTIFICALLY

In this book, you'll find a range of experiments and investigations that will help you discover how evolution and classification work.

To do experiments, scientists use careful, logical methods to make sure they get reliable results. The experiments in this book use four key scientific methods, along with an easy acronym to help you remember them: A**T**O**M**.

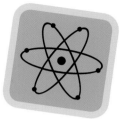

 ## ASK

What do you want to find out?
Asking questions is an important part of science. Scientists think about the questions they have, and how to find answers.

 ## TEST

Setting up an experiment that will test ideas and answer questions
Scientists design experiments to answer questions. Tests work best if you only test for one thing at a time.

OBSERVE

Key things to look out for
Scientists watch their experiments closely to see what is happening.

 ## MEASURE

Measuring and recording results, such as temperatures, sizes, or amounts of time
Making accurate measurements and recording the results shows what the experiment has revealed.

WHAT NEXT?

After each experiment, the What Next? section gives you ideas for further activities and experiments, or ways to display your results.

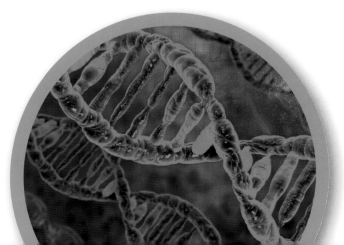

EVOLUTION IN ACTION

In the 1800s, Charles Darwin (1809–1882) and Alfred Russel Wallace (1823–1913), discovered how evolution worked.

The two scientists studied similar living things, **fossils**, and the way farmers change plant and animal species by breeding them. They saw how one species could gradually turn into another or become several new species. Charles Darwin studied birds called finches on the Galápagos Islands near South America. He saw that the different species were similar, but had different beaks for eating different types of food. Darwin realized they must have all evolved from an earlier species.

These are some of the finches that Charles Darwin (top) studied.

THE PEPPERED MOTH

Darwin and Wallace figured out how evolution must have happened in the past. But in the 1900s, scientists realized we could *see* it happening, too. In Europe, a species called the peppered moth began to change its **camouflage** as smoke pollution from factories made tree trunks and walls darker. Most peppered moths were pale, but a few were dark.

As pollution made surfaces darker, the pale moths were easier to spot against a dark background and birds ate more of them. Meanwhile, more dark moths survived.

The dark moths lived longer and had more babies. Over time, the species became mainly dark. It had evolved to suit its new habitat.

pale peppered moth on a tree

Which of these two peppered moths would be easier for a bird to spot?

YOU WILL NEED:

- A computer, printer, and paper
- Scissors
- Timer
- At least 2 players

SCIENCE EXPERIMENT:
MOTH MODEL

This experiment is a model — a recreation of a real-life situation that works in the same way.

Moths are a favorite food for lots of birds.

ASK

How does evolution cause a species to change color over several **generations**?

TEST

- Use the Internet to find photos of paler and darker tree trunks and rocks. Print out several large images.
- Cut 10 dark and 10 pale moth shapes from some of the pictures.
- Pick one player to be the "bird."
- While the "bird" looks the other way, arrange the dark and pale moths on one of the pale backgrounds.
- Give the "bird" 5 seconds to find and pick up as many moths as possible.
- Try the same test again, but on a darker background.

OBSERVE

Does the "bird" find poorly camouflaged moths faster?

MEASURE

After each test, how many moths of each color are left behind to survive?

WHAT NEXT?

Do some research to find out if the peppered moth has changed again since its environment is cleaner now and has less smoky pollution.

Polluting smoke from factory chimneys was a common sight in the 1800s and early 1900s.

SURVIVAL OF THE FITTEST

You may have heard the phrase "survival of the fittest." It dates from 1864, when another scientist, Herbert Spencer (1820–1903), used it to describe Charles Darwin's ideas.

Today, "fit" can mean strong or healthy. However, in the term, "survival of the fittest," it means the most *suitable*. The living things that survive best are the ones that fit, or suit, their habitat the best.

So when species evolve, they don't simply get stronger or bigger — they become better **adapted**, or suited, to their habitat. They evolve the most useful features to help them survive.

Herbert Spencer was a famous scientist in the 1800s.

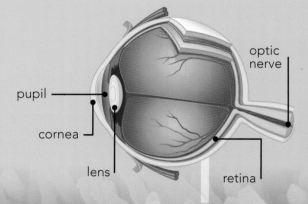

pupil
cornea
lens
optic nerve
retina

HOW DO YOU SURVIVE?

In the modern world, it might seem easy for humans to survive. But, like other living things, we have evolved all kinds of useful features to help us stay alive. For example, our eyes are good at noticing movement, which helps us avoid dangers such as an angry animal or a speeding car.

Our bodies tell us when we are hungry or thirsty, and our sense of smell warns us when something is burning. And we have evolved large brains and skilled hands that allow us to invent, make, and use all kinds of tools.

The human eye has many parts that work together so that we can see well. A human retina contains millions of light-sensitive rods and cones.

rod
cone

YOU WILL NEED:

- Several people
- A ground floor window
- Cotton balls

SCIENCE EXPERIMENT:

REFLEX TESTS

Human and other living things have reflexes, or automatic reactions. Reflexes have evolved because they are useful features that help us to stay safe and to deal with danger. These experiments test two of your reflexes.

ASK

How do reflexes protect your body and help it survive?

TEST

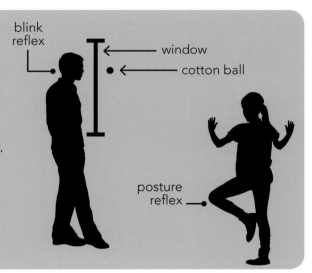

- To test the blink reflex, one person should stand behind a window. Their face should be as close to the window as possible.
- From the other side, throw cotton balls at their face so that the balls hit the window in front of their eyes.
- To test **posture** reflexes, ask the same person to balance on one leg.
- Gently push the person, so that they wobble but do not fall over.
- Repeat the tests with another person.

OBSERVE

How do people react when you carry out the test? How do their reflex movements protect them or help them? Is it different in different people?

MEASURE

Do some people have faster or slower reflexes than others?

WHAT NEXT?

Think about how these two reflexes could help you survive, especially in **prehistoric** times. What dangers or threats could they protect against?

The blink reflex makes you blink when water splashes on your face.

FINDING FOOD

Living things have evolved ways of finding the best food to help them survive, and avoiding what's bad for them.

A tiger drinks the fresh water flowing in a stream.

For example, many wild animals prefer to drink from running water in a stream. If possible, they avoid stagnant, still water, such as in a muddy pond. This is because running water is less likely to contain dirt and germs.

When wolves kill **prey**, they always eat the **organs** and **bone marrow**. Polar bears go for a seal's **blubber**. These animals prefer these parts because they contain the most **calories**, **proteins**, or essential **vitamins**.

Polar bears feast on a seal, their favorite food.

FAVORITE FOODS

Humans are similar. We've evolved preferences for foods that contain lots of calories, such as high-fat and high-sugar foods. This is because in prehistoric times, sugary and fatty foods were essential for survival. We can also tell when food has gone bad by its smell or appearance. We find it disgusting — and that helps us to survive by avoiding food poisoning.

Humans find rotting food, like this moldy sandwich, gross!

YOU WILL NEED:

- A computer, printer and paper
- A group of people
- Pen and paper

SCIENCE EXPERIMENT:

DELICIOUS OR GROSS?

Test your friends' tastes and reactions to reveal which things humans have evolved to find appealing and which we find disgusting.

Ask

How do human reactions reveal how evolved preferences protect us?

Test

- Use the Internet to collect pictures of different foods, such as celery, cabbage, doughnuts, pizza, chocolate, bananas, and yogurt, and pictures of moldy bread, vomit, and grass. Print the pictures.
- Show 5–10 people the pictures and ask them to rate each one from 1 (for disgusting) to 10 (for delicious).

Facial expressions often reveal how people feel.

Observe

How do people react to the pictures? Look for facial expressions and body movements. Write down their ratings.

Measure

Add up the scores. Which pictures scored highest and lowest?

WHAT NEXT?

Make a simple graph to display your results, ranking the pictures in order from the most appealing to the most disgusting.

Can you see a pattern? Even though we no longer have to survive in the same harsh conditions as our prehistoric ancestors, many people still like to eat sugary and fatty foods. Can you think how this evolved preference could harm our bodies?

ADAPTING TO HABITATS

Each living thing has evolved and adapted to its own habitat, where it lives, feeds, and survives.

For example, a spider monkey lives in rainforest trees. It has a **prehensile tail** for curling around branches, and hands and feet with fingers and toes that are good at holding branches and picking fruit.

A spider monkey uses its tail to grip onto branches.

A mole lives in underground tunnels. It has poor eyesight, but a very sensitive nose for finding food, and big, powerful front claws for digging.

European mole

EVOLUTION EVERYWHERE

Around the world, **biologists** find that where living things have to deal with the same types of habitats and conditions, they tend to evolve similar features. Sometimes this happens even if they are not close relatives. This is called **convergent evolution**.

LOSING LEGS

Today's whales evolved from small, four-legged animals. Although they once had legs, they gradually lost them. A smooth body with flippers at the front suited life in the water better. Over time, the back legs shrank away.

pelvis and hindlegs

These two **mammal** species look very similar. They have both evolved to glide from trees using loose, thin skin that they can spread out like wings. But they are very different — the sugar glider is a **marsupial** related to kangaroos, and the flying squirrel is a **rodent** related to squirrels and rats.

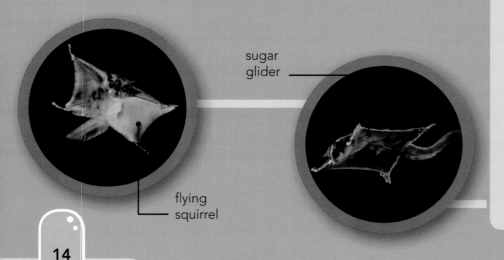

sugar glider

flying squirrel

SCIENCE EXPERIMENT:
CREATURE FEATURES

— fennec fox

Predict which kinds of features go with each of the habitats, then check your predictions against the answers. Scientists check their predictions by making observations in the field.

ASK

What features do you think animals will adapt for particular habitats?

OBSERVE

How do you decide which goes where?

TEST

• Research and print out photographs of three habitats: a snowy forest, a hot, sandy desert, and the open ocean.
• Look at the set of creature features below and list the five features you think would be most useful in each habitat.
  • big ears
  • big feet
  • blowhole
  • burrowing claws
  • closeable nostrils
  • flippers
  • furry feet
  • golden fur
  • inflatable body parts
  • sharp claws
  • small ears
  • thick fur
  • torpedo-shaped body
  • triangle-shaped tail
  • white feathers

MEASURE

Check your predictions against the answers on page 32. How many of them did you get right?

WHAT NEXT?

Compare the features to those that humans have. Why do you think we don't have fur, sharp teeth, or big claws?

FINDING A MATE

The way species change over time can only work because living things reproduce, or have babies, and pass on their features to them. The main reason one animal has more babies than another is because it survives better and lives longer.

However, there's another way to have more babies, and that's to be the best at finding a **mate**. Many species have features that help them do this, such as the male peacock's tail.

Male peacocks with the biggest and brightest tails are more likely to attract peahens (females) to mate with. Over time, peacocks and many other species have evolved features like these for impressing potential mates, as well as survival features. This is called **sexual selection**.

A male peacock's tail feathers have beautiful "eye" patterns.

A male peacock displays his tail to a passing peahen.

YOU WILL NEED:

- Several people
- Shoe boxes or shoe box lids
- Blue paper, art materials, and other objects
- Twigs or wooden popsicle sticks
- Scissors
- Glue, sticky tape, or modeling clay

SCIENCE EXPERIMENT:
BEAUTIFUL BOWERS

Male satin bowerbirds build a bower (a kind of shelter or enclosed area) to impress a mate. Each male decorates his bower with blue objects — feathers, flowers, berries, or even blue pieces of litter. Hold your own bower-building contest to see who is best at winning a mate.

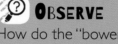

ASK

How do bowerbirds make their bowers attractive?

OBSERVE

How do the "bowerbirds" try to make their bowers the most attractive?

TEST

- Appoint one person to be the female bowerbird, who will judge the bowers.
- Give each contestant some time to collect blue decorative objects and materials at home or around the classroom.
- Each contestant should then build a bower from sticks in their shoe box or lid, and decorate it with blue objects.
- Without knowing who made which bower, the female bowerbird should award points for style, color, and shape, and select the most appealing bower.

MEASURE

Who was the winner? What type of decorations got the most points?

WHAT NEXT?

Research the things real bowerbirds do to make their bowers pretty, such as arranging rows of objects in size order from smallest to largest. Can you find out how some other animals display to attract a mate?

A male bowerbird works on perfecting his bower.

GENES AND GENETIC TRAITS

We know that evolution happens because of the way living things pass on their individual features to their babies. But how exactly does this work?

Living things are made up of tiny parts called cells. They have babies, or reproduce, using special reproductive cells. In plants, the reproductive cells make seeds. In animals, reproductive cells make eggs or babies. Tiny single-celled bacteria reproduce by splitting in two, making two new cells.

Dandelions pass on their features inside the seeds they produce.

E. coli bacterium pass on their features by dividing in two.

Chickens pass on their features to chicks in the eggs female chickens lay.

GENES

Cells, including reproductive cells, contain **genes**, which are made of a spiral-shaped chemical called **DNA** (see page 26). Genes control how a living thing grows and what it looks like. When living things reproduce, they give their offspring copies of their own individual genes in their reproductive cells. This is how features, such as a rabbit's strong back legs or a peacock's big tail, get passed on.

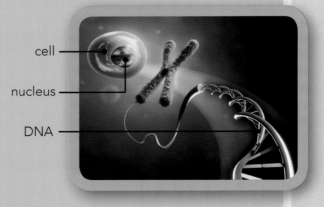

cell

nucleus

DNA

A cell's DNA is in its nucleus.

SCIENCE EXPERIMENT:
TOE TEST

Features passed on in your genes are called **genetic traits.** They include things like hair color, height, and shapes of body parts. Children get genes from both their parents and often share some genetic traits with them. In this experiment, you can test for a genetic trait called Morton's toe.

ASK

Are biological family members more likely to share a genetic trait than people who aren't related?

TEST

- Test yourself and your friends and family for Morton's toe. If you have it, your second toe is longer than your big toe.
- Each person should make a list of their family members, and a list of the same number of unrelated friends.
- They should then ask them all if they have Morton's toe.

This diagram shows a foot with Morton's toe.

This diagram shows a foot without Morton's toe

OBSERVE

Are family members more likely to have the same kind of toes than friends?

MEASURE

How much difference is there between the two groups?

WHAT NEXT?

Make two pie charts, one for the group of unrelated friends, and one for the family group, to show the frequency of Morton's toe. You could also combine everyone's results and make a graph to see if they show a pattern.

Repeat the test, but this time compare earlobes. Find out if each person has dangling earlobes, which hang down separately from their head, or attached earlobes, which join to the side of the head at the bottom.

CLASSIFICATION

Life has existed on Earth for at least 3.5 billion years. In that time, millions and millions of different species have evolved. Scientists classify every new species they discover, working out which groups and categories it belongs to.

ONE BIG FAMILY

Scientists think all life evolved from one original life form, which means that all living things are related. Living things *all* work and grow using cells, genes, and DNA.

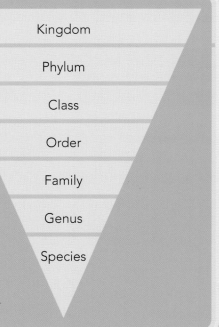

Because species branch off from other species, some are very closely related, and others are much more distantly related. Monkeys are close relatives of humans. Octopuses are more distant relatives, and bananas are really distant relatives.

HOW CLASSIFICATION WORKS

The classification of a species looks a bit like an upside-down pyramid. It shows the categories that a species belongs to. For example, the largest group in this pyramid is a kingdom, such as the animal kingdom, which includes all animals. Animals are divided into over 30 phyla, or main groups. Each phylum can be separated into classes, orders, and families, genuses or specific types, and finally individual species.

Look at the simple classification tree on page 23 to see how several branches of kingdom, phylum, and class are connected.

| Kingdom |
| Phylum |
| Class |
| Order |
| Family |
| Genus |
| Species |

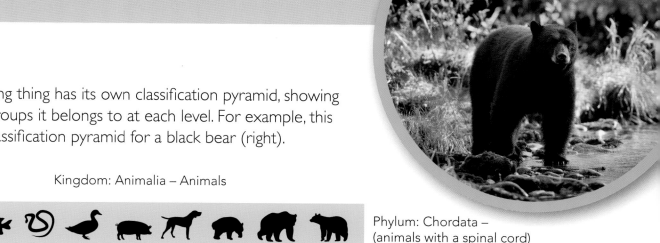

Each living thing has its own classification pyramid, showing which groups it belongs to at each level. For example, this is the classification pyramid for a black bear (right).

Kingdom: Animalia – Animals

Phylum: Chordata – (animals with a spinal cord)

Class: Mammalia – Mammals (warm-blooded animals that have hair and breathe air)

Order: Carnivora – Carnivores (animals that feed on other animals)

Family: Ursidae – Bears (includes the panda, brown bear, black bear, and other bears)

Genus: *Ursus* – (includes the brown bear and black bear)

Species: *Ursus americanus* – black bear

GETTING IT RIGHT

Sometimes scientists classify a living thing in one category, then change their minds as they find out more about it. The giant panda is an example of this. In the past, it was thought to belong to the raccoon family. Studies revealed it is more closely related to bears like the black bear, and belongs in the bear family, Ursidae.

giant panda

raccoon

SCIENCE EXPERIMENT:
CLASSIFY THIS!

Can you draw and fill in classification pyramids for these three living things using your own research?

coconut palm tree

ladybug

human

21

SORTING IT OUT

How do scientists know which living things to put where in the classification system? They look at many different things, including the way a living thing breathes, what it eats, its body shape, its limbs, how it reproduces, and whether it has fur, feathers or **scales**.

Swan:
Class: Aves, Family: Anatidae, Genus: *Cygnus*

American robin:
Class: Aves, Family: Turdidae, Genus: *Turdus*

For example, the class Aves, or Birds, is one of the classes in the Animal Kingdom. All birds have beaks, feathers, and two legs. They lay hard-shelled eggs and have wings (though not all birds can fly).

Blue-footed booby:
Class: Aves, Family: Sulidae, Genus: *Sula*

IS IT A BIRD?

If a scientist discovers an animal with these features, it's definitely a bird and belongs in Aves. To work out its family and genus, the scientist would then look at more of the bird's detailed features and compare it with other birds to see which it was most similar to (see the three examples above).

Sometimes, biologists also study and compare the DNA of living things (see left) as a way to find out how closely related they are.

THIS DOESN'T FIT!

If scientists discover a living thing that doesn't fit into any existing category, they sometimes have to create a new category. This means the classification system is always growing and changing.

SCIENCE EXPERIMENT:
BE A BIOLOGIST

Sort out the living things into the right categories in the classification tree. You might have to do some research to find out the features of each category.

ASK

How do you decide which categories a living things belongs in?

CATEGORIES
• amphibians
• arachnids
• birds
• cephalopods
• crustaceans
• fish
• flowering plants
• gastropods
• insects
• mammals
• non-flowering plants
• reptiles

TEST

• Look at each of the living things below and see if you can work out which category each belongs in (without checking on the Internet!). The categories are listed on the right and a simplified diagram of the classification tree is below to help you.

  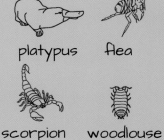 

axolotl   rose   platypus   flea   octopus   penguin

sea turtle   slug   scorpion   woodlouse   seahorse   moss

Hints: the word "gastropod" comes from the Greek for "stomach-foot." The word "cephalopod" comes from the Greek for "head-foot."

OBSERVE

How do you make your decisions? Which creatures are the most difficult to classify?

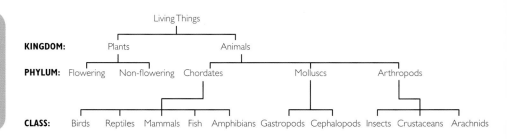

MEASURE

How many did you get right? The answers are on page 32.

WHAT NEXT?

Do some research to find out about new species that have only been discovered in the last ten years. What kind of living things are they?

BODY PLANS

Have you ever noticed that some animals seem to share human features? A monkey, a rat, and a squirrel all have hands a bit like ours that can hold food. You can often tell how a dog feels from its facial expression, just like you can with a human friend.

Because living things evolve from other living things, they often share similar features. Even animals that are very different and belong to separate groups or categories often have a similar body plan.

Shark skeleton

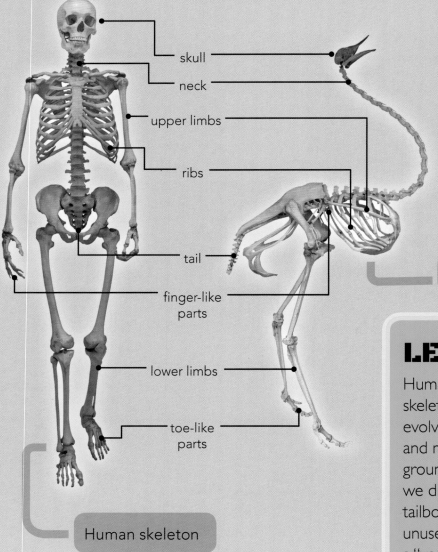

skull

neck

upper limbs

ribs

tail

finger-like parts

lower limbs

toe-like parts

Human skeleton

MATCHING PARTS

For example, humans and birds are very different, but their skeletons show that they have the same basic body plan.

Ostrich skeleton

LEFTOVER TAIL

Humans don't have tails, but our skeletons have a tailbone. As we evolved from monkey-like animals and moved from the trees to the ground, our tails shrank because we didn't really need them. The tailbone is all that is left. A leftover, unused body part like this is called a "vestigial" part.

SCIENCE EXPERIMENT:
LIVING RELATIVES

When you look at different animals' skeletons, their body plans can reveal how closely related they are. Scientists use this to help classify some types of living things.

ASK Can skeletons reveal which species are our closest relatives?

A crab's skeleton is its hard shell and it is on the outside of its body. It is called an exoskeleton.

TEST

- Look at the animal skeletons below.
- Which do you think is our closest relative, and why?

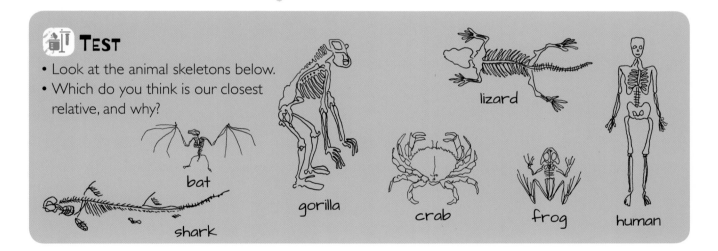

bat

shark

gorilla

lizard

crab

frog

human

OBSERVE

Look for similarities in body structures and parts. Can you spot parallels to our hands, arms, or legs in some of the skeletons and not others?

WHAT NEXT?

Look up more animal body shapes and skeletons. Can you find out which is our closest animal relative of all?

MEASURE

Can you arrange the skeletons in order of how closely they are related to humans? You can find out if you were right on page 32.

A frog's skeleton is made up of 159 bones. A human skeleton has 206 bones.

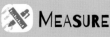

THE DNA KEY

Evolution "selects" the most useful features in living things. This can only happen because living things are all slightly different, even within the same species. That's because each individual has its own unique set of genes inside its cells.

COPYING ERRORS

Genes are made of the chemical DNA. When cells divide or living things reproduce, the DNA is copied so that new cells can be made. As this happens, changes called mutations can occur in the copies. These mutations make each individual slightly different.

To copy itself, a strand of DNA separates into two halves. Each half builds up a new other half, making two new full strands.

It's possible to see strands of DNA with the naked eye when they are removed from their cells.

Ask an adult to use the rubbing alcohol. Never use it by yourself or put it in your mouth, as it can be dangerous.

YOU WILL NEED:

- Freezer
- Rubbing alcohol (as close to 100% alcohol as possible)
- A banana and a fork
- Liquid soap • Water
- Bowl • Sieve
- A teaspoon and a tablespoon
- A tall glass or jar

SCIENCE EXPERIMENT:

DNA FROM A BANANA

DNA is found in the cells of living things, including food plants. It's normally inside the cells, but this experiment lets you release it and see it.

Ask

How can you extract DNA from a banana?

Test

- First, ask an adult to put the rubbing alcohol in the freezer for a day to get it really cold.
- Peel the banana, put it in the bowl, and mash it well with the fork.
- Add 2 teaspoons of liquid soap and 2 tablespoons of water and stir in gently.
- Leave the mixture for 10 minutes, then use a spoon to push it through the sieve and collect the liquid in the glass.
- Ask an adult to gently pour in the same amount of cold rubbing alcohol as there is liquid in the glass and leave for 20 minutes.

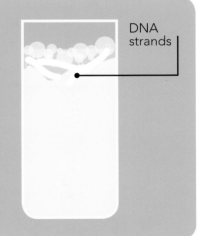

DNA strands

Observe

After 20 minutes, there should be a white, lumpy substance at the top of the liquid. This is the DNA. Use the fork to lift bits out.

Measure

DNA is string-shaped (see page 26), but the strings often coil up into lumps. How long are the longest strings you can see?

WHAT NEXT?

Find out how long all the DNA in a human body would be if it were all stretched out.

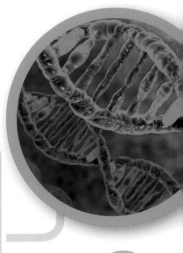

The 3-D shape of DNA is called a double helix. The word "helix" comes from the Greek word for "twisted" or "curved."

READING YOUR RESULTS

When scientists do experiments, they get results. Even if nothing happened as they expected, that is a result too! All results can be useful, but it is important to understand them. Here are some guidelines that scientists use to learn from their results.

USE A CONTROL

In the Toe Test experiment on page 19, the group of unrelated friends is the control. A control is a normal version of the setup, without the thing that is being tested. So if you are testing a group of relatives, you need to compare it with another group, who are not related to each other.

Apart from the thing being tested, the control version must match the test version in every way. For example, both groups must have the same number of people in them. Then you know that any differences in your results are down to one group being related.

REPEAT AND VERIFY

An experiment may work well once, but what if that was a fluke? So that they can be sure of their results, scientists often repeat an experiment several times to verify their results.

CHECK FOR BIAS

If you're *really* hoping for an exciting result, it's possible you might accidentally-on-purpose "help" your experiment along by ignoring something that doesn't fit with what you wanted. This is called "bias," and it can happen without you even realizing it.

OUTLIERS

What if you were conducting the Delicious or Gross experiment on page 13, and one of your test subjects gave vomit a rating of 10 out of 10 for deliciousness?

This would be very unexpected and hard to explain. This kind of unusual result is called an outlier. When scientists find outliers, they have to think about whether to discount them from the experiment, or change their experiments to include them. In this case, it might be that the person doing the test didn't understand the rating system. You might decide to double-check this and try again.

KEEPING RECORDS

Writing down the details of each experiment and what the results were is essential for scientists. Not only does it help explain their work to others; it also means they can use results to look for patterns. For example, you might find that the DNA from a Banana experiment on page 27 works better with very ripe bananas, or with unripe ones.

MAKING MISTAKES

If you spot a mistake, start the experiment again. It would be an even bigger mistake to use the results from a badly run experiment.

However, if a mistake makes something interesting happen, you could set up a new experiment to test for that instead. Important discoveries have been made this way. For example, sticky notes were invented when an inventor was trying to make extra-strong glue, but accidentally created a very weak glue instead.

GLOSSARY

adapt To change to become well-suited to a habitat.

amphibian A cold-blooded animal with a backbone. They usually breathe through gills as young and breathe air as adults.

bacteria A type of tiny single-celled living thing.

biologist An expert in biology.

biology The study of life and living things.

blubber The thick layer of fat found under the skin of some sea animals, such as seals.

bone marrow The soft, fatty substance inside large bones.

calories Units of energy, which are used to measure the amount of energy contained in food.

camouflage Markings, shapes, or colors that blend in with the surroundings.

classification Sorting living things out into different types, groups, and species.

convergent evolution Evolution of similar traits or features in living things that are not closely related.

DNA (deoxyribonucleic acid) The long, spiral-shaped chemical that genes are made from.

evolution A process of gradual change over steps or generations.

extinct No longer existing.

fossil Rock that has formed the shape of a long-dead living thing or its bones

generation A group of living things that live at the same time. Their children are the next generation, their grandchildren are the generation after that, and so on.

genes Sections of DNA containing instructions that tell cells what to do and control how a living thing grows and works.

genetic trait A feature that is passed on from parents to children by genes.

geology The study of rocks and the Earth.

germs Tiny organisms that cause disease.

habitat The natural home or surroundings of a living thing.

in the field When scientists study in wild or natural environments, rather than in a lab.

Latin The language of ancient Rome and its empire. It is widely used in science.

mammal A warm-blooded animal with a backbone that breathes air, has hair, and drinks its mother's milk when it is young.

marsupial A mammal that grows inside a pouch on its mother's body when it is very young.

mate Mating happens when a male and female living thing meet to join their reproductive cells together in order to reproduce. A "mate" also means an animal that another animal mates with.

natural selection The way features that help living things to survive are selected by evolution.

organ A body part, such as the heart or liver, which performs a job.

posture The way in which you hold your body when standing or sitting; a pose.

predator A living thing that hunts and eats other living things.

prehensile tail A tail that can hold or hang onto objects.

prehistoric From the time before history was written down.

prey A living thing that is eaten by another living thing.

protein An essential part of the diet of many living things that helps build strong muscles and other body parts.

reflex An automatic body reaction that has evolved to help a living thing survive.

reproduce To have babies or offspring so that a species can continue.

reptile A cold-blooded animal with a backbone that usually has dry, scaly skin.

rodent A small mammal with sharp teeth for gnawing, such as a rat or squirrel.

scales Hard plates that overlap to protect the skin of reptiles and some fish.

sexual selection The way features that help living things to win a mate are selected for by evolution.

species The scientific name for a particular type of living thing.

virus A type of tiny germ that can cause some types of diseases.

vitamin An essential part of the diet of many living things, which provides a special type of nutrition and helps growth.

BOOKS

Evolution: The Whole Life on Earth Story by Glenn Murphy (Macmillan)

What is Evolution? by Louise Spilsbury (Wayland)

Evolution Revolution Dr Robert Winston (Dorling Kindersley)

The Story of You by Anna Claybourne (Wayland)

Living Processes: Animal Variation and Classification by Carol Ballard (Wayland)

Straightforward with Science: Classification and Evolution by Peter Riley (Franklin Watts)

WEBSITES

PowerKids Press has developed an online list of websites related to the subject of this book. This site is updated regularly. Please use this link to access the list:

www.powerkidslinks.com/tyss/evolution

INDEX

ANSWERS

p.15. CREATURE FEATURES:

Hot, sandy desert: big ears • burrowing claws • closeable nostrils • furry feet • golden fur
Open ocean: blowhole • flippers • inflatable body parts • torpedo-shaped body • triangle-shaped tail
Snowy forest: big feet • sharp claws • small ears • thick fur • white feathers
Don't worry if your answers don't match these ones, sometimes there is more than one right answer. Here are some examples:
- Closeable nostrils are used by some desert animals to keep sand out of their noses, but they are also used by marine mammals, such as seals, when they dive underwater.
- Some desert animals have fur on the bottom of their feet to protect their feet from hot surfaces, but polar bears also have furry feet to protect their feet from cold surfaces.
- Camels have big feet that help them walk on soft sand. Snowshoe hares also have big feet compared to the size of their bodies. Their big feet help spread their body weight and stop them from sinking into deep snow.

p. 23. BE A BIOLOGIST:

amphibians: axolotl • arachnids: scorpion • birds: penguin • cephalopods: octopus • crustaceans: woodlouse • fish: seahorse • flowering plants: rose • gastropods: slug • insects: flea • mammals: platypus • non-flowering plants: moss • reptiles: sea turtle

p. 25. LIVING RELATIVES:

The order of our animal relatives from closest to furthest is: gorilla, bat, lizard, frog, shark, crab.